THE UNDERGROUND RAILROAD

Raymond Bial

Houghton Mifflin Company
Boston 1995

This book is respectfully dedicated to the workers on the Underground Railroad who daily risked their lives to help others and to those who continue to carry forward the flickering light of liberty.

Copyright © 1995 by Raymond Bial

Library of Congress Cataloging-in-Publication Data

Bial, Raymond.
    The underground railroad / Raymond Bial.
       p.   cm.
    ISBN 0-395-69937-1
    1. Underground railroad—Juvenile literature. 2. Fugitive slaves—
United States—History—19th century—Juvenile literature.
I. Title.
E450.B53   1995   94-19614
973.7'115—dc20   CIP
                         AC

Printed in Singapore

TWP 10 9 8 7 6 5 4 3 2 1

Foreword

Because the Underground Railroad had to operate in deep secrecy, many basic facts about its history are unknown. No one knows exactly how many men and women were involved in the railroad or how many fugitives were assisted by those committed to the cause.

Certainly, tens of thousands of slaves, aided by more than 3,200 railroad "workers," escaped to the northern states and Canada, and today scores of little towns from Maine to Iowa have their secrets about the railroad. It's usually a story talked about at the café or a footnote in a local history book about a runaway who was hidden in an old barn at the edge of town; the child who slipped under a bed when the slave catcher knocked on the door; the husband and wife who held their breath in the attic while the sheriff searched for them downstairs; or the house up the street with a tunnel through which fugitives were smuggled out late at night. Passed down through the generations, the stories are as varied as the people who worked with the Underground Railroad in those years before the Civil War when slavery was not only tolerated but upheld by law.

It was important to me to visit these places, not just to make photographs but to stand on the very ground of the slave cabins where men, women, and children were held in bondage, to gaze on the courthouse yard where human beings were auctioned off to the highest bidder, to wander through the antebellum homes that served as "stations" on the Underground Railroad where fugitives were hidden from bounty hunters. I was deeply impressed that significant events, both terrible and heroic, actually happened in these very places, and I was left with a feeling of reverence for those brave people—both runaways and workers on the Railroad—who had gone before us.

Photography had not yet been invented when many of the daring actions of the Underground Railroad occurred, and all of the workers have long since passed away. Yet I believed I could accurately capture the spirit of drama in these otherwise quiet places—both the courage of flight and the nobility of the aid extended to fugitive slaves. It seemed that I could really feel the presence of these people, and I have attempted to re-create faithfully the atmosphere of the woods, the gleaming river, and the purple cast of the night sky along with the tingle of anticipation, the utter terror of being pursued, and that glimmer of promise offered by the yellow light in an upstairs window.

Many of the photographs in *The Underground Railroad* were made late at night and far from my home. As you page through this book, imagine yourself, as I did, being hunted down as you struggle through a thick and unfamiliar woods or wade through a treacherous swamp. Also imagine yourself being helped by kind people along the way because, despite the cruelty and injustice of slavery, one cannot live without hope and faith in other people. The worst of times always brings out the very best in some people, and such is the story of the Underground Railroad.

THE UNDERGROUND RAILROAD

Many routes of the Underground Railroad crossed the Ohio River, which bordered several free states, notably Ohio, Indiana, and Illinois. Runaways swam, waded, or rowed across the river on their own or were assisted by conductors on the Underground Railroad.

"If you come to us and are hungry, we will feed you; if thirsty, we will give you drink; if naked, we will clothe you; if sick, we will minister to your necessities; if in prison, we will visit you; if you need a hiding place from the face of the pursuer, we will provide one that even bloodhounds will not scent out."

— *Credo of the American Anti-Slavery Society, 1843*

Tice Davids broke for the woods, dodging trees and tangled bushes, trying desperately to get away; his furious master was right behind him. When Tice came to the Ohio River, he plunged into the water without a moment's hesitation. Not taking his eyes off Tice, his master jumped into a skiff and rowed after the runaway, who was swimming for his life. Tice had barely gotten to the other side near Ripley, Ohio, when his master also touched land, but the runaway slave had vanished. The slave owner searched everywhere but couldn't find a clue. Thoroughly baffled, he concluded, "He must have gone on an underground road!"

This is just one story of how the Underground Railroad got its name. Later, when railroads began to crisscross the country, the network of escape routes became known as a "railroad." In another version of the story, seventeen runaways were well hidden in the attic of Levi Coffin's house in Newport (later Fountain City), Indiana. Frustrated slave hunters complained, "There's an Underground Railroad around here, and Levi Coffin is its president!"

The Underground Railroad was, in fact, an informal yet intricate network of routes leading north, eventually to Canada. The vast system extended from Maine to Iowa, with routes in Pennsylvania, Ohio, and Indiana the most heavily traveled. Ohio was literally crisscrossed with the invisible lines of the railroad. Not actually underground, the railroad ran through woods, over fields, and across rivers, most often operating under cover of darkness. The name added to the mystery because the railroad ran without trains or rails. Escaping slaves followed the North Star or were directed to a specific safe house or "station" just across the border of a free state. Once in a northern state, fugitives were assisted and led from one station to the next by railroad workers. Runaways were transported in coaches, trains, steamships, and skiffs, but most often in wagons or on foot.

By 1830 the Underground Railroad was well established, yet no one knew the entire system because it had to operate in such secrecy. The less one knew, the less one could reveal. Because of the dangers involved, records were seldom kept and others were destroyed. The railroad was most active in the sixty years before the Civil War, when there were over 3,200 workers on the railroad, many of whom were blacks. It is estimated that five hundred escaped slaves returned south each year to "conduct" other blacks to freedom.

No one is certain of the origin of the Underground Railroad. Vestal Coffin, cousin of Levi Coffin, and his wife, Althea, may have started it in Guilford County, North Carolina, and the first line may have been through Indiana. But every home that welcomed run-aways and every individual who offered food, clothing, or other assistance could be considered part of the railroad.

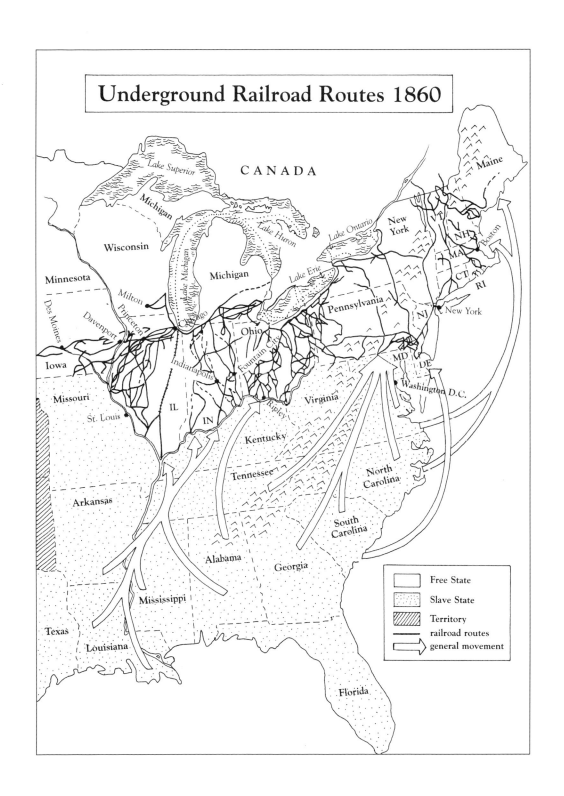

Underground Railroad Routes 1860

CANADA

Lake Superior

Michigan

Wisconsin

Lake Huron

Lake Michigan

Michigan

Lake Ontario

New York

Minnesota

Milton

Des Moines

Davenport

Princeton

Chicago

VT

NH

MA

CT

RI

Boston

Iowa

Indianapolis

Ohio

Fountain City

Pennsylvania

NJ

New York

Missouri

St. Louis

IL

IN

Ripley

Virginia

MD

DE

Washington D.C.

Kentucky

Arkansas

Tennessee

North Carolina

Alabama

South Carolina

Georgia

Mississippi

Texas

Louisiana

Florida

	Free State
	Slave State
	Territory
	railroad routes
	general movement

Hidden away in a barn behind the Levi Coffin House in Indiana, this wagon had a false bottom beneath which runaway slaves could be hidden under sacks of grain while being driven to the next station.

Some courageous men and women ventured south to encourage slaves to run away. These "pilots" gave directions and spread word of the railroad. "Conductors" undertook the most dangerous work; they actually led slaves north, often to Canada, because even in a free northern state, runaways weren't safe. By law they were property and could be returned to their masters. Conductors either led "passengers" on foot or hid runaways in wagonloads of straw or vegetables. Homes, churches, and schoolhouses served as hiding places called "stations," "depots," or "safe houses," operated by "stationmasters." Escaped slaves might be hidden literally underground in cellars or tunnels, as well as in attics, fake closets, or secret rooms. In addition to shelter, the railroad's "cargo" was given food and clothing and, if needed, care for broken bones, cuts—and sometimes bullet wounds.

A secret hand-dug tunnel connected the Milton House, a Wisconsin inn, with a log cabin. Hidden in the tunnel, runaways waited in silence, their only light a candle or oil lamp.

Workers on the Underground Railroad came from all walks of life. Some were ministers like Owen Lovejoy and John Rankin, others businessmen like Quaker Levi Coffin. One worker, Gerrit Smith, was a millionaire who ran twice for President of the United States. Most were ordinary people—shopkeepers and farmers—who quietly did what they thought was right. Not formally organized, the Underground Railroad grew out of people's concern for others and was made up of both black and white people working closely together. Many of the blacks had themselves been slaves who, in an expression of personal courage, wished to help others to freedom.

Runaway slaves could carry little food and had to make their journey weakened by hunger. Exposed to the weather, huddled

Slaves lived in very humble circumstances, especially when compared to the mansions in which the masters lived. Located on the Carter Gove Plantation near Williamsburg, Virginia, this fine home was built largely by slave labor.

Slaves wisely chose to slip away from their cabins at night. They not only avoided detection but had a whole night's head start before the overseer discovered they had run away and turned the dogs loose.

against the cold and rain, they traveled through unfamiliar country-side, often guided only by the North Star, which they had heard would lead them across the Ohio River to the free states of Ohio, Indiana, and Illinois or from Maryland and Virginia into Pennsylvania. Runaways might also stow away on paddleboats churning up the Mississippi River or hide aboard ships plying up the Atlantic coast from the cities of Norfolk and Portsmouth in Virginia to ports in New York, Boston, or Providence, Rhode Island. The methods of escape were as varied and as ingenious as the thousands of men, women, and children who sought their freedom. Often, these runaways were helped and gradually a network of routes and safe houses developed.

As shown in this illustration of Tom and Simon Legree from *Uncle Tom's Cabin*, slaves lived under the threat of the whip usually administered by a mean-spirited overseer who punished slaves at the slightest hint of resistance. (*Courtesy Illinois Historical Society Library*)

Capturing runaways became a lucrative business after the Fugitive Slave Law was enacted in 1793. This law permitted a master or professional bounty hunters, called slave catchers, to seize runaways, even in a free state. Slave catchers haunted the roads all the way from Georgia to Lake Erie, earning their living hunting down

These shoes probably did not provide much comfort to the slave who wore them. But imagine the desperate fugitive who had to run for his life through the woods and fields in bare feet.

runaways and returning them for rewards. Many professional slave catchers had bloodhounds, often called "Negro dogs," specially bred to follow the scent of fugitives. In 1849 a slaveholder in Mississippi boasted about his slave catcher: "He follows a negro with his dogs 36 hours after he has passed and never fails to overtake him. It is his profession and he makes some $600 per annum at it." Slave catchers didn't always care if they got the right person, and in response vigilance committees were formed to resist the kidnapping of free blacks. Rachel Parker, a free black, was captured and told to confess that she belonged to a Mr. Schoolfield or else, she related, her captor "would cowhide me and salt me, and put me in a dungeon. I told him I was free, and that I would say nothing but the truth."

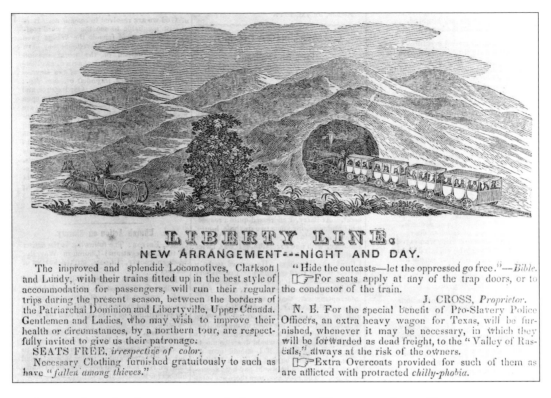

LIBERTY LINE.

NEW ARRANGEMENT---NIGHT AND DAY.

The improved and splendid Locomotives, Clarkson and Lundy, with their trains fitted up in the best style of accommodation for passengers, will run their regular trips during the present season, between the borders of the Patriarchal Dominion and Libertyville, Upper Canada. Gentlemen and Ladies, who may wish to improve their health or circumstances, by a northern tour, are respectfully invited to give us their patronage.

SEATS FREE, *irrespective of color.*

Necessary Clothing furnished gratuitously to such as have "*fallen among thieves.*"

"Hide the outcasts—let the oppressed go free."—*Bible.*
☞For seats apply at any of the trap doors, or to the conductor of the train.

J. CROSS, *Proprietor.*

N. B. For the special benefit of Pro-Slavery Police Officers, an extra heavy wagon for Texas, will be furnished, whenever it may be necessary, in which they will be forwarded as dead freight, to the "Valley of Rascals," always at the risk of the owners.

☞Extra Overcoats provided for such of them as are afflicted with protracted *chilly-phobia.*

Workers on the railroad sometimes used advertisements. This appeared in a Chicago newspaper called *The Western Citizen* in July, 1844. *(Courtesy Illinois Historical Society Library)*

Local sheriffs, other slave owners, and people who believed in obeying the law—as well as other slaves hoping for a reward from the master—often caught or reported fugitive slaves.

In Canada, however, black men could vote and hold public office as well as sit on juries and live anywhere they wished. Over time, thriving communities developed in Windsor, Ontario, and elsewhere. In 1842 Josiah Henson, a runaway and conductor, established the Dawn Institute in Dresden, Ontario, where former slaves could learn trades and live independently. So many runaways found their way to Canada that in 1826 plantation owners petitioned Secretary of State Henry Clay to negotiate a plan with Canada to return runaways. The Canadian government refused to consider the idea.

In the United States, the Quakers were the first group to actively help runaway slaves. Following the Biblical passage "Thou shalt not deliver up to his master the servant which hath escaped unto thee" (Deut. 23:15), they assisted runaways from the time America was an independent nation. As early as 1786 George Washington complained that "a society of Quakers, formed for such purposes, have attempted to liberate" one of his slaves. In 1794 the Society of Friends, as the Quakers were called, declared that it was wrong "to live in ease and plenty by the toil of those whom fraud and violence had put in their power."

$150 REWARD.

RANAWAY from the subscriber, on the night of Monday the 11th July, a negro man named

TOM,

about 30 years of age, 5 feet 6 or 7 inches high; of dark color; heavy in the chest; several of his jaw teeth out; and upon his body are several old marks of the whip, one of them straight down the back. He took with him a quantity of clothing, and several hats.

A reward of $150 will be paid for his apprehension and security, if taken out of the State of Kentucky; $100 if taken in any county bordering on the Ohio river; $50 if taken in any of the interior counties except Fayette; or $20 if taken in the latter county.

july 12-84-tf   B. L. BOSTON.

This wanted poster shows not only how runaways were hunted down like outlaws, but also how they were treated by their masters. Note the description of the whip marks. (*Courtesy Ohio Historical Center*)

These chains were used to hobble slaves, especially those determined to escape to freedom. At other times, slaves were shackled together to make it difficult, if not impossible, for them to run away.

Similarly, many workers on the railroad considered the Declaration of Independence their manifesto: "We hold these truths to be self-evident—that all men are created equal; that they are endowed by their Creator with certain inalienable rights; that among these are life, liberty, and the pursuit of happiness." When the United States was established, however, slavery was an entrenched part of life. America was the first successful democracy, yet a significant number of its people had no rights. Thus began a contradiction at the very inception of the nation.

The "rights" of slave owners were even written into the Constitution. Although the word "slave" does not appear, Article IV, clause 2, became known as the "fugitive slave and felon clause." Adopted in 1787, it read in part: "No person held to service or labor in one state, under the laws thereof, escaping into another, shall, in consequence of any law or regulation therein, be discharged from such service or labor, but shall be delivered up on claim of the party to whom such service or labor may be due." When many states refused to return runaways, the 1793 Fugitive Slave Law was passed, making it a crime to help a fugitive. Canada became an important destination as runaways were never entirely safe in free states.

Finally, in 1808, Congress outlawed the importation of slaves. The slave trade continued in the West Indies and South America, however, and some Africans were still smuggled into the United States. By this time, many slaves had already been born in the country that, despite the conditions in which they lived, had become their home. They had become Americans as well as Africans.

Slaves lived in cabins like this one at Carter's Grove Plantation. The cabins were like those of white pioneers, but poorly furnished.

Slave auctions were held in the courthouse yard on Main and North Court streets in Washington, Kentucky. When Harriet Beecher Stowe visited here in 1833, she witnessed an auction and was inspired to write *Uncle Tom's Cabin*.

By the early 1800s, the northern states along the Atlantic seaboard had outlawed slavery, and the Northwest Ordinance of 1787 had already provided that all states in the Midwest, as far as the Mississippi River, would enter the Union as free states. The south became slave states, and after the cotton gin was invented, in 1793, slaves were in even greater demand in the Deep South, where this crop was grown. Slaves in Kentucky, Virginia, Maryland, and other border states could be "sold south" for high prices, and slaves trembled at the prospect of having to work as field hands for fourteen hours a day, seven days a week, in intense heat, always under the lash of an overseer.

Slaves became most desperate to run away if they were about to

Not all escapes were successful. Many were caught and punished. Treated as criminals, they could be held in jails, including this one in Williamsburg, Virginia. The prisoners slept on a bed of straw, and the only light came through the small barred window in the door.

be sold, which often happened when death or financial difficulties caused the breakup of an estate. Slaves also escaped from situations of cruel abuse. According to Wilbur Siebert, of all the "passengers" on the Underground Railroad "none brought a back so shamefully lacerated by the lash as Thomas Madden. Not a single spot had been exempted from the excoriating cow-hide. A most bloody picture did the broad back and shoulders of Thomas present to the eye." Another slave's biography described the "life and narrative of William J. Anderson, twenty-four years a slave; sold eight times! in jail sixty times! whipped three hundred times!!!" Most slaves fled from border states such as Kentucky, Virginia, and Maryland, although many attempted the long journey from the Deep South.

Slaves were not allowed to learn to read, and it was illegal to educate them. Further, slave marriages were not recognized by law and families could be callously broken up at sales. Fugitive slave John Brown (not the white abolitionist) recalled these auctions: "Here may be seen husbands separated from their wives, only by the width of the room, and children from their parents, one or both, witnessing the driving of the bargain that is to tear them asunder forever, yet not a word of lamentation or anguish must escape from them; nor when the deed is consummated, dare they bid one another good-bye, or take one last embrace. Even the poor, dear, little children, who are crying and wringing their hands after 'daddy and mammy,' are

Families were often broken up at auctions. Here a father is being sold while the anguished mother and child await their fate on the auction block. (*Courtesy Illinois Historical Society Library*)

22

not allowed to exchange with them a parting caress. Nature, however, will not be thus controlled, and in spite of the terrors of the paddle and the cowhide, the most fearful scenes of anguish and confusion often take place."

Brown also described his own parting: "At last we got to the gate, and I turned around to see whether I could not get a chance of kissing my mother. She saw me, and made a dart forward to meet me, but Finney [the slave trader] gave me a hard push, which sent me spinning through the gate. He then slammed it to and shut it in my mother's face. That was the last time I ever saw her, nor do I know whether she is alive or dead at this hour."

A group of men forcibly separate a mother from her child. She will be sold at auction, never to see her child again. *(Courtesy Illinois Historical Society Library)*

TO BE SOLD & LET

BY PUBLIC AUCTION,

On MONDAY the 18th of MAY, 1829,

UNDER THE TREES.

FOR SALE,

THE THREE FOLLOWING

SLAVES,

VIZ.

HANNIBAL, about 30 Years old, an excellent House Servant, of Good Character.
WILLIAM, about 35 Years old, a Labourer.
NANCY, an excellent House Servant and Nurse.

The MEN Belonging to "LEECH'S" Estate and the WOMAN to Mrs. D. SMIT.

TO BE LET,

On the usual conditions of the Hirer finding them in Food, Clothing and Medical Attendance,

THE FOLLOWING

MALE and FEMALE

SLAVES,

OF GOOD CHARACTERS,

ROBERT BAGLEY, about 20 Years old, a good House Servant.
WILLIAM BAGLEY, about 18 Years old, a Labourer.
JOHN ARMS, about 18 Years old.
JACK ANTONIA, about 40 Years old, a Labourer.
PHILIP, an Excellent Fisherman.
HARRY, about 27 Years old, a good House Servant.
LUCY, a Young Woman of good Character, used to House Work and the Nursery.
ELIZA, an Excellent Washerwoman.
CLARA, an Excellent Washerwoman.
FANNY, about 14 Years old, House Servant.
SARAH, about 14 Years old, House Servant.

Also for Sale, at Eleven o'Clock,

Fine Rice, Gram, Paddy, Books, Muslins, Needles, Pins, Ribbons, &c. &c.

AT ONE O'CLOCK, THAT CELEBRATED ENGLISH HORSE

BLUCHER,

ADDISON PRINTER GOVERNMENT OFFICE.

This announcement for a public sale includes slaves to be sold and others to be "let" or hired out to the highest bidder. Considered property, slaves were treated no differently from the various merchandise and the horse offered for sale. *(Courtesy Levi Coffin House)*

Josiah Henson recalled a similar experience from his childhood: "My brothers and sisters were bid off first and one by one, while my mother, paralyzed by grief, held me by the hand." When Josiah was offered for sale, his mother fell to the ground before the master "and clung to his knees, entreating him in tones that a mother only could command, to buy her baby as well as herself and spare to her one, at least, of her little ones." But the master "disengaged himself with such violent blows and kicks that she was forced to creep out of his reach and mingle groans of pain with the sobs of a breaking heart."

Virtually every slave longed to be free, and the "plantation grapevine" became an effective means of communication. Slaves also sent messages through songs. Having converted to Christianity, they created their own spirituals, or "sorrow songs," using the words as a kind of code. Harriet Tubman, who conducted many runaways to the "promised land," acquired her nickname, "Moses of Her People," from the song "Go Down Moses." In this song "Egypt's land" is the south and "Pharaoh" is the slaveholder.

> When Israel was in Egypt's Land,
> Let my people go.
> Oppressed so hard they could not stand,
> Let my people go.
> Go down, Moses, way down in Egypt's Land,
> Tell old Pharaoh, let my people go . . .
> No more shall they in bondage toil,
> Let my people go.
> Let them come out with Egypt's spoil,
> Let my people go.

Slaves generally slept on a bed of straw on the floor with little more than a rough quilt or thin blanket to cover themselves. They were allowed few possessions and had little time in which to provide for themselves.

Stationmaster Levi Coffin remembered one woman's escape from a plantation in Mississippi: "One night, when all around her were wrapped in sleep, she put a small supply of food and some clothing together, in a little bundle, and, stealing away from the negro quarters, left the plantation and plunged into the forest, which was there a labyrinth of swamps and cane-breaks. She made her way through this slowly, for several days, often hearing the bloodhounds baying on her track, or perhaps in search of other fugitives. Slaves often fled to these swamps and took refuge among the thickets, preferring the companionship of the deadly moccasin snake and the alligator, and the risk of death from starvation or exposure to the cruel treatment of their masters, and the keen cut of the overseer's lash.

26

"This slave woman managed to evade the dogs by wading in pools and streams of water, where she knew they would lose the scent and be thrown off her trail. One time, however, she heard the deep baying of the bloodhounds coming toward her when she was some distance from any water. There was no escape and she knew they would soon come up with her and tear her to pieces before the pursuers could reach them." When the dogs approached, however, "she took from her pocket a handful of crumbs—the remainder of the food she had brought—and held them out toward the hounds. They came up to her, but instead of seizing and mangling her, they gamboled about her, licked the crumbs from her hands, then ran off through the forest . . . She had a long journey after that, lasting for several months,

Runaway slaves often took to the water to throw the dogs off their scent. Desperate to be free, they crossed rivers at night and waded through marshes thick with snakes in the hours before dawn.

Standing high upon Liberty Hill in Ripley, Ohio, the home of John and Jean Rankin offers an excellent view of the Ohio River and the state of Kentucky. The house was ideally located for helping runaways make their way from slavery to freedom.

and encountered many dangers, but was preserved safe through them all. She traveled at night and hid in thickets during the day, living mostly on fruit and green corn, but venturing now and then to call at negro huts and beg for a little of the scanty food which they afforded . . . Reaching Illinois, she met with kind people who aided her on to Detroit, Michigan. Here also she found friends and was ferried across to Canada."

Not all attempts to secure freedom were successful. Stationmaster John Rankin recalled a black man he sheltered who escaped to Canada and then returned to Kentucky for his wife and two children. After a long journey, he picked his way through the woods by the plantation. After dark he got word to his wife and the family fled

The Rankins placed a light in an upstairs window to signal runaways that slavecatchers were not lurking about town and it was safe to approach their home.

toward the Ohio River. As soon as their flight was discovered, the master sent a slave catcher after them. The slave catcher soon caught up with them and grabbed one child who had fallen behind. Forced to abandon the child, the parents got across the Ohio River, but were ambushed by the slave catcher the next day. The mother and children were returned to the plantation and the father was sold south, never to see his family again.

With the ever-present danger of capture, hiding places assumed great importance. Levi Coffin began helping slaves when he was a young man in North Carolina and later recalled, "Runaway slaves used frequently to conceal themselves in the woods and thickets of New Garden, waiting opportunities to make their escape to the

Built in 1839, the Levi Coffin House was strategically located about twenty miles north of the town of Liberty, Indiana, another station on the railroad. With three railroad routes converging on the town, hundreds of runaways were sheltered in this home in the years before the Civil War.

North, and I generally learned their places of concealment and rendered them all the service in my power. These outlying slaves knew where I lived, and, when reduced to extremity of want or danger, often came to my room, in the silence and darkness of the night, to obtain food or assistance."

When he moved to Newport, Indiana, in 1826, a hundred runaways passed through his red brick home each year on their way to Canada. His basement was used as a hiding place, and a horse and wagon were kept in readiness. Coffin recalled, "We knew not what night or hour of the night we would be roused from slumber by a gentle rap at the door . . . Outside in the cold or rain, there would be

The space under the eaves of the Levi Coffin House was regularly used to hide runaway slaves. Once runaways had slipped through the entry, the door was closed and the bed was pushed in front of it.

a two-horse wagon loaded with fugitives, perhaps the greater part of them women and children. I would invite them, in a low tone, to come in, and they would follow me into the house without a word, for we knew not who might be watching and listening."

Among the many people who helped fugitive slaves was Pennsylvanian Thomas Garrett, who offered food and shelter to about 2,500 runaways. In 1848 he was arrested for breaking the Fugitive Slave Law. He was forced to sell all his property to pay the huge fine and was left destitute, yet he told the sheriff who conducted the auction of his life's possessions, "Friend, I haven't a dollar in the world, but if thee knows a fugitive anywhere on the face of the earth who needs a breakfast, send him to me."

Born to a slaveholding family in Virginia, John Fairfield became one of the most active conductors on the Underground Railroad. He became especially adept at rescuing the wives and children of slaves who had found freedom in the north. It was very dangerous for black conductors to go into the slave states, so they worked mainly in the north. Able to pose as a Negro trader, slaveholder, or peddler, Fairfield made numerous trips to the south, rescuing several hundred slaves before he died in 1860 during a slave revolt in Tennessee.

Abolition was still a very unpopular cause and when people such as Levi Coffin and John Rankin spoke out against slavery they were often met with a barrage of rotten eggs, spoiled vegetables, and rocks. In 1837 Elijah P. Lovejoy, an editor who published an abolitionist newspaper called the Alton *Observer,* was killed in Alton, Illinois, a small town along the Mississippi River, while protecting his printing press from a proslavery mob. But abolitionists persevered.

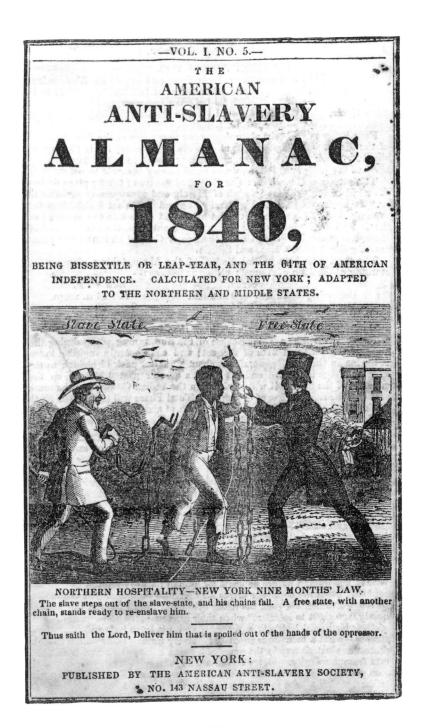

The American Anti-Slavery Almanac was used by abolitionists to draw attention to the desperate conditions under which slaves lived and to generate public outrage against the cruelty of slavery. (*Courtesy Indiana Historical Society Library*)

Runaways were hidden behind a fake wall in the eaves of the attic at the Owen Lovejoy Homestead in Princeton, Illinois. The opening was concealed behind a large chest of drawers.

By the soft glow of candlelight at this desk, Owen Lovejoy wrote many fiery sermons about the cruel injustice of slavery, which he then delivered to his congregation. He told them, "I shall preach this doctrine 'till you like it, and then I shall preach it because you like it."

Reverend Owen Lovejoy, brother of Elijah Lovejoy and friend of Abraham Lincoln, openly preached against slavery from the pulpit and, when elected to Congress, declared: "Owen Lovejoy lives at Princeton, Illinois, three quarters of a mile east of the village, and he aids every fugitive that comes to his door and asks it . . . Let it echo through the arches of heaven, and reverberate and bellow along the deep gorges of hell, where slave catchers will be very likely to hear it. Thou invisible demon of slavery, dost thou think to cross my humble threshold and forbid me to give bread to the hungry and a shelter to the homeless! I bid you defiance in the name of God."

Fugitives were more likely to trust a free black. So, despite the extreme danger, black men such as John Mason, Josiah Henson, and J. W. Loguen, who was called "King of the Underground Railroad," returned south as conductors. John Parker, a free black who owned a foundry in Ripley, Ohio, was just one of an estimated five hundred black conductors. Parker often rowed across the Ohio River at night to help runaways over the wide expanse of water and even ventured into Kentucky to guide runaways. One of the white employees at his foundry dared Parker to get away with any of the slaves on his father's Kentucky plantation. Despite the postings of "Reward $1000 for John Parker, Dead or Alive," Parker traveled to the plantation's slave quarters. One couple was desperate to escape, but the master

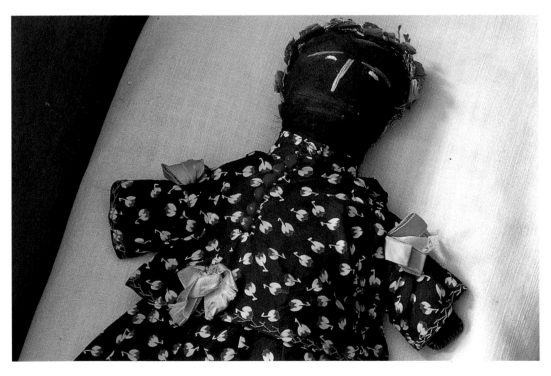

Katie Coffin, the wife of Levi Coffin, gathered women in her home to sew clothing for runaways and to make dolls to comfort their children as they fled through the night.

This view from the John Rankin House shows the Ohio River with a light in the distance. Runaways made their way across the river from Kentucky to sanctuary in the Rankin home.

had their baby sleep at the foot of his bed, where he kept a lighted candle and a loaded pistol.

Parker asked the couple to describe the house's interior; then he waited until dark. Taking off his shoes, he crawled into the bedroom and scooped up the baby. He knocked the candle and pistol off the table with a throw of the baby's pillow, and before the slave owner could find a light, Parker was running with the baby and parents to a waiting boat. When they were about halfway across the river, shots rang out and Parker had the couple lie down in the boat. Rowing hard, he not only got the passengers across the river but safely transferred them to another conductor before their former master reached the shore.

The venerable Harriet Tubman, an escaped slave herself, could not read or write, yet by age thirty she was notorious as a conductor. She made nineteen trips to Maryland. "God willed us free," she said. "Men willed us slaves. We will do as God wills."

When she was about to be sold south, never to see her family again, she recalled, "I had reasoned this out in my mind; there was only one of two things I had a right to, liberty or death; if I could not have one, I would have the other; for no man should take me alive; I should fight for my liberty as long as my strength lasted . . ." Once she reached the free state of Pennsylvania, she said, "I looked at my hands to see if I was the same person. There was such a glory over everything. The sun came up like gold through the trees, and I felt like I was in heaven." Although slaveholders placed a $12,000 reward on her head, she was never caught.

Frederick Douglass, who escaped from slavery in 1838, gave a clear, resounding voice to the abolitionist movement. An eloquent speaker and writer, Douglass often began his speeches, "I appear before you as a thief and a robber. I stole this head, these limbs, this body from my master and ran away from him." Everywhere he went, Douglass forced people to ask themselves how such a refined, intelligent speaker could be considered "property." He dared to speak out at a time when free blacks were tormented and could be kidnapped and sold back into slavery. In the very first issue of the *North Star*, an antislavery newspaper Douglass published, he declared his involvement in the Underground Railroad. The following railroad "pass" was written by Douglass: "My Dear Mrs. Post: Please shelter this Sister from the house of bondage till five o'clock—this afternoon— She will then be sent on to the land of freedom. Yours truly, Fred K."

As Harriet Tubman guided runaways through the black of night, she must certainly have found comfort in the warm yellow light shining from the windows of the homes that served as stations of the Underground Railroad.

LET THE NORTH AWAKE !!

T. B. M'CORMICK

Will discuss the Immorality, Illegality and Unconstitutionality of

AMERICAN SLAVERY,

And the Duty and Power of the General Government to Abolish it,

ON_____EVENING_____ AT_____ O'CLOCK,

IN THE_____

Mr. M'Cormick, formerly of Kentucky, is the Clergyman for whom the Governor of Kentucky made a Requisition upon the Governor of Indiana, charging him with aiding in the escape of Fugitive Slaves. The Warrant was issued, and Mr. M'Cormick is thereby exiled from home. All are respectfully invited to attend.

Abolitionist Thomas B. McCormick was so active in assisting runaways that the governor of Kentucky requested that he be extradited. To avoid arrest McCormick had to flee to Canada himself. *(Courtesy Indiana Historical Society Library)*

The antislavery movement became so successful that millions of dollars worth of "property" was escaping, and "owners" demanded a new, tougher Fugitive Slave Law. Not one in ten southerners owned slaves, but most people benefited from the system. And northerners prospered from the peculiar institution as well: cotton and other agricultural products were supplied to northern factories, and finished goods were in turn sold in the south. These goods included clothing, hats, and shoes—even the whips used to punish slaves. Some storekeepers, such as Levi Coffin, sold only "Free Labor Goods," which indicated that they were made without the use of slave labor.

Because the activities of the Underground Railroad had to be kept secret, it is now difficult to know exactly the extent of its work, but the railroad nonetheless became a testament to the disgrace of slavery. Some historians claim that its impact has been overstated, but the passage of the Fugitive Slave Law and the alarm of slaveholders are clear indications that the railroad not only threatened but

PUBLIC NOTICE.

THIS day was committed to the custody of the Sheriff of Randolph county, State of Illinois, as Runaway, a Negro Man who calls himself

Martin Barker,

about forty-three years of age, about five feet nine inches high, a scar over his right eye, and also one on his right leg above his ancle, his make and his appearance active ; he states that he once belonged to Lewis Barker, of Pope county near the Rock-in-Cave but that he is now free. If any person has any legal claim to him, they are requested to exhibit the same and pay all charges, according to law.

ANT. DUFOUR, *D. Sheriff*
For Thos. J. V. Owen. S R C.
Kaskaskia, Dec. 11, 1826   21-6t

Although he was detained in a free state and claimed to be free, Martin Barker was held and this notice published in the *Illinois Reporter* newspaper so that he could be returned to anyone with "legal claim to him." (*Courtesy Illinois Historical Society Library*)

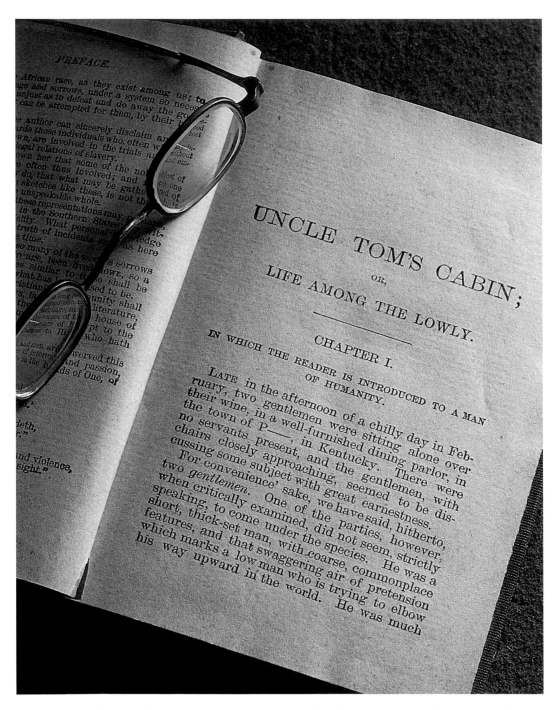

Uncle Tom's Cabin stirred many people into action, and at least one copy of the book found a place in the Lovejoy home. Two of the principal characters, Eliza and Tom, were based on actual runaways whom the Rankins and their thirteen children aided.

damaged the institution of slavery. In 1850 Congress passed a more severe Fugitive Slave Law, which made it easier for slave catchers to capture free blacks by stating that any dispute would be settled, not by jury, but by a commissioner who was paid $5.00 if he decided in favor of the black and $10.00 if he decided for the master.

Thomas Sims became the first fugitive to be sent back to slavery under the new law. Transported to Savannah, Georgia, on a ship chartered by the United States government, he was publicly whipped, then imprisoned for two months, after which he was sold. Years later, during the Civil War, he was freed by Union forces near Vicksburg, Mississippi. During the 1850s, of more than three hundred blacks detained in the north, including many free blacks, all but eleven were sent to southern masters.

Many people were incensed by the injustice of this law. Then, in 1851, Americans began to read Harriet Beecher Stowe's *Uncle Tom's Cabin*, a novel that vividly depicted the cruelty of slavery, and another wave of indignation swept across the country. Three hundred thousand copies of the book were sold in the first year, and eight presses were kept running, day and night, to keep up with the demand. Many people now insisted that the law be changed and slavery ended altogether.

In the late 1850s, a wild-eyed abolitionist named John Brown devised an extreme plan to free the slaves—he would attack the United States arsenal at Harpers Ferry, West Virginia, and thereby incite a slave rebellion throughout the south. Harriet Tubman advised him to carry out the revolt on July 4, but the event that would further shape American opinion occurred on October 16-17, 1859, when Brown led a small band of twenty-two men, seventeen of whom were white, on what was obviously a doomed mission. Federal troops led by Colonel Robert E. Lee crushed the attack, killing ten men, including Brown's son.

Before being hanged for treason, Brown spoke eloquently: "I believe that to have interfered as I have done, as I have always freely admitted I have done, in behalf of [God's] despised people, I did no wrong but right." Brown's attack graphically demonstrated how divided the nation had become over slavery.

Barely a year after Harpers Ferry, the people of the United States elected a lanky young man from Illinois as the President of a deeply torn nation. Although stating that he was opposed to immediate abolition, Abraham Lincoln had often debated the grievous wrong of slavery. Immediately upon his election, the state of South Carolina announced its secession from the Union. By Lincoln's inauguration most southern states had seceded and the new President suddenly found himself leader of only half a nation. It was the beginning of the Civil War.

Slaves living in the Confederate States were freed when the Emancipation Proclamation was enacted on January 1, 1863. At the conclusion of the Civil War, slavery was formally abolished in the United States when the Thirteenth Amendment of the Constitution was ratified on December 18, 1865. The work of the Underground Railroad was completed, yet the struggle for equality for all Americans continues to this very day.

Chronology of the Antislavery Movement in America

1775   The first abolitionist society was organized by Benjamin Franklin in Philadelphia, a year before the Declaration of Independence was adopted.

1793   The Fugitive Slave Law was passed, making it a crime to assist an escaped slave and permitting masters or slave catchers to seize runaways, even in free states.

1808   Congress prohibited the importation of Africans, although slaves were still smuggled into the United States and the slave trade within the country, especially between the border states and the Deep South, was further developed.

1820   The Missouri Compromise enacted, which attempted to maintain the balance between the number of slave and free states. Maine was admitted as a free state and Missouri entered the Union as a slave state. Slavery was also forbidden in the northern territories of the Louisiana Purchase.

1831   William Lloyd Garrison, the fiery editor of the *Liberator*, and eleven other whites formed the New England Anti-Slavery Society.

1833   The American Anti-Slavery Society was established in Philadelphia, with three blacks among its founders.

1850   The Compromise of 1850 permitted California to be admitted as a free state and the territories of New Mexico and Utah were allowed to decide whether to be free or slave, but it also included a stricter Fugitive Slave Law.

1854   The Kansas-Nebraska Act went into effect, providing that these two territories would decide by "popular sovereignty" whether to enter the Union as free or slave states. The act was directly contrary to the Missouri Compromise and led to bloody warfare in the territories.

1857   The Dred Scott case determined that slaves were not citizens and could not bring suit in the courts. Dred Scott was returned to his master in Missouri.

1859   John Brown's raid brought to public attention the desperate need to end slavery.

1860   The election of Abraham Lincoln was followed by the secession of South Carolina, Alabama, Florida, Georgia, Louisiana, Mississippi, Texas, and other southern states.

1863   The Emancipation Proclamation freed the slaves in all the rebel states.

1865   The Thirteenth Amendment of the Constitution was ratified, abolishing slavery in the United States.

Further Reading

Many excellent books are available in libraries and bookstores for those who would like to read more about the Underground Railroad. Along with primary sources, the following books were consulted in the preparation of this book.

Blockson, Charles. *The Underground Railroad*. New York: Prentice Hall, 1987.

Buckmaster, Henrietta. *Let My People Go: The Story of the Underground Railroad and the Growth of the Abolition Movement*. Boston: Beacon Press, 1941.

Campbell, Stanley W. *The Slave Catchers: Enforcement of the Fugitive Slave Law*. Chapel Hill, N.C.: University of North Carolina Press, 1968.

Coffin, Levi. *Reminiscences of Levi Coffin: The Reputed President of the Underground Railroad*. New York: Augustus M. Kelley Publishers, 1968.

Crenshaw, Gwendolyn J. *Bury Me in a Free Land: The Abolitionist Movement in Indiana, 1816–1865*. Indianapolis: Indiana Historical Bureau, 1993.

Finkelman, Paul, ed. *Fugitive Slaves*. New York: Garland Publishing, Inc., 1989.

Gaines, Edith M. *Freedom Light*. Cleveland: New Day Press, 1991.

Gara, Larry. *The Liberty Line: The Legend of the Underground Railroad*. Lexington, Ky.: University of Kentucky Press, 1967.

Kolchin, Peter. *American Slavery: 1619–1877*. New York: Hill & Wang, 1993.

Nichols, Charles H., ed. *Black Men in Chains*. New York: Lawrence Hill & Co., 1972.

Siebert, Wilbur H. *The Underground Railroad from Slavery to Freedom*. New York: Arno Press, 1968.

Still, William. *The Underground Railroad*. Chicago: Johnson Publishing Co., 1970.

Young people may also be interested in these books about the Underground Railroad.

Cosner, Shaaron. *The Underground Railroad*. New York: Franklin Watts, 1991.

Haskins, Jim. *Get On Board: The Story of the Underground Railroad*. New York: Scholastic, 1993.

White, Anne Terry. North to Liberty: *The Story of the Underground Railroad*. Champaign, Ill.: Garrard Publishing Co., 1972.

Only recently has it been recognized that blacks had a history and that their heritage is interwoven, north and south, into the cloth of American culture. There are still too few historical sites that offer interpretive programs about black Americans, and these places are often difficult to find. The following two books proved to be very helpful to me and may be recommended to anyone wishing to visit places important in the history of black Americans.

Thum, Marcella. *Exploring Black America: A History and Guide*. New York: Atheneum, 1975.

Thum, Marcella. *Hippocrene U.S.A. Guide to Black America*. New York: Hippocrene Books, 1991.

Acknowledgments

Just as the operation of the Underground Railroad depended upon the goodwill and hard work of others, many people gave generously of themselves in making this book.

Among the many people who provided advice and direction are Glennette Tilley Turner, Cheryl Kennedy, and John Hoffmann. Mary Michals of the Illinois Historical Society Library supplied a wonderful selection of illustrations for the book as did the staff at the Indiana State Museum, the Indiana Historical Society Library, and the Ohio Historical Center.

I would like to thank the following people who assisted me in photographing at important historical sites: Curtia James and Rosemarie Byrd (Colonial Williamsburg), Ezby Collins (Owen Lovejoy Homestead), Sandra Jackson (Levi Coffin House), Judy Sheehle (Milton Museum), and Lobena Frost and Bernard Cooper (John Rankin House). These people patiently gave of their time, often early in the morning or well into the evening, as I peered through the viewfinder of my camera trying to take that one rare, elusive photograph.

I would like to thank the staff at Houghton Mifflin for their strong support of this book, most especially Matilda Welter, who suggested the subject, and Audrey Bryant, who carefully and ably guided the work to completion.

As always, I would like to thank my wife, Linda, and my dear children, who endured my absences while I was out taking photographs.